LAMB a cookbook

LAMB a cookbook

LAMB

a cookbook

By

Colin Simpson

© 2018 Cape Neddick Cookbooks
4th Edition

ISBN-13: 978-1511787574
ISBN-10: 1511787570

DEDICATION

This book is dedicated to my mother-in-law Bee Jay Gallant – Happy 80th Birthday!!!

TABLE OF CONTENTS

About the book

About the author

Introduction

The recipes

About The Book

Dear Friends!

Welcome to Lamb-a-cookbook, the latest in my series showing that meals cooked at home can be simple, healthy and delicious. Lamb is an excellent addition to the series, as it is a meat that is rich in nutrients and full of flavor.

A 3 ounce serving of trimmed lamb has only 175 calories, and provides almost 5 times the omega-3 fatty acids and alpha linoleic acid as a 3 ounce serving of beef. Lamb provides twice the amount of iron as chicken or pork and six times more than fish. Both American and Australian lamb are an all-natural product, raised without growth hormones, making lamb a good protein choice.

This book features over 50 of my favorite lamb recipes for everyone in the family to enjoy. From Lamb Burgers to Lamb and Shrimp Kebabs to Roast Leg of Lamb, we have every occasion covered with tried and perfected recipes.

We hope you enjoy these delicious lamb recipes as much as our family and friends do.

Happy healthy cooking,

Colin Simpson.

About the author

Colin is a professional cook and former restaurateur who resides on the beautiful coast of Southern Maine in New England. From the moment he was the first male to take cooking classes in his high school in Edinburgh, Scotland, Colin has not stopped developing his passion for cooking. Having travelled extensively, his constant focus has been learning new recipes and cooking techniques around the globe.

Colin's first cookbook **Salmon a cookbook** became a best seller within a week of its release. Colin has always enjoyed sharing his tasty dishes with family and friends and now as a successful author he continues to write to share his favorite recipes with a wider audience.

Colin's 'a cookbook' series:

SALMON a cookbook
LAMB a cookbook
CHICKEN BREAST a cookbook
Soup of the Day

http://www.amazon.com/Colin-Simpson/e/B00DYQNMGG

Introduction

Good organization is key to successful cooking, to avoid mistakes and save time. I have a simple process I use with all recipes which is probably similar to yours, but thought I would share it with you.

After reading the entire recipe through, I ensure all my ingredients and utensils are laid out in place. I pre-heat the oven if required and then do all the prep, following the recipe instructions in the listed order. When ready to cook, I set the timer. Being prepared makes cooking easy, more fun and saves time!

When you choose your cut of lamb, ask the butcher to trim it for you. Trimming removes the fat and will make the lamb cook more evenly, not to mention making it a healthier choice.

The recipes are displayed so you never need to turn a page. There is even space at the end of the recipes for you to write your own notes.

LAMB

a cookbook

The Recipes:

Stout Braised Lamb Shanks

Prep: 25 min - Cook: 2 hours - Serves Six

Ingredients:

6 lamb shanks - about 1 lb. each - trimmed

5 cups chopped onions

4 cups beef stock

2 12oz. bottles Guinness stout

4 carrots – peeled - cut into 1 inch pieces

2 large parsnips – peeled - cut into 1 inch pieces

2 rutabagas – peeled - cut into 1 inch pieces

1/2 cup prunes - pitted

1/2 cup all-purpose flour

1/3 cup vegetable oil

1 tablespoon fresh thyme

1 tablespoon fresh parsley

2 teaspoons fresh rosemary

2 bay leaf

Kosher salt and fresh ground black pepper

Directions:

1. Heat vegetable oil in a large skillet, over high heat.

2. Season lamb with salt and pepper, then coat with flour. Reserve rest of flour.

3. Add lamb to hot oil in skillet and brown well, about 5 minutes. Remove lamb, set to side, and reduce heat to medium.

4. Add the chopped onions to skillet and sauté until translucent, about 5 minutes. Add reserved flour and stir 1 minute, then add beef stock, Guinness, thyme, parsley, rosemary and bay leaf. Stir well and bring to a boil, then add lamb. Reduce heat, cover and simmer for an hour.

5. Add carrots, parsnips and rutabagas to skillet and simmer uncovered for 40 minutes. Spoon fat from surface of stew, add prunes and simmer uncovered another 20 minutes, or till vegetables are tender.

Mashed potato and green beans compliment this dish.

Herb Roasted Butterflied Leg of Lamb

Prep: 15 min - Cook: 65 min - Serves Six

Ingredients:

3 lb. butterflied leg of lamb – trimmed

2 cloves garlic - cut into slivers

Kosher salt and fresh ground black pepper

Combine the following ingredients in a small bowl:

1/4 cup olive oil

3 tablespoons fresh parsley - chopped

2 tablespoons fresh rosemary - chopped

1 tablespoon fresh thyme - chopped

2 tablespoons orange juice

1 tablespoon orange zest

Directions:

1. Combine the bowl ingredients, set to side.

2. Poke the lamb with a tip of a knife, and insert garlic slivers. Evenly spread the herb mix over top of lamb, place in roasting pan then season lamb with salt and pepper.

3. Roast the lamb in a **preheated 425 degree oven** for 20 minutes, then **reduce oven heat to 350 degrees**. Cook till desired tenderness. Medium rare – about 45 minutes.

4. Remove roast lamb from oven and slice before serving.

Make gravy from the drippings, and serve with roast potato and your choice of vegetable.

Tandoori Lamb Steaks

Prep: 10 min - Cook: 10 min – Marinate: 2 hours - Serves Four

Ingredients:

4 Lamb sirloin steaks - trimmed

1 tablespoon olive oil

Kosher salt

ground black pepper

Marinade: combine the following ingredients in a blender:

1/2 cup plain yogurt

1/4 cup heavy cream

1/2 cup cilantro

1 small red onion

3 tablespoons curry powder

Directions:

1. Trim lamb steaks.

2. Season lamb steaks with salt and pepper. Put lamb steaks and marinade into a bowl, cover and refrigerate for 2 hours or overnight.

3. Heat oil in skillet over high heat and add marinated lamb steaks. Sear on both sides till charred and pink in the middle, about 8 minutes total.

4. Serve immediately.

Basmati rice, chutney, green beans and poppadums complete this dish.

Moroccan Lamb Tagine

Prep: 30 min - Marinate: 6+ hours – Cook: 2 hours - Serves Six+

Ingredients:

2½ lb. lamb – trimmed - cut into 1½ inch chunks

2 14oz. cans diced tomatoes

2 cups tomato juice

2 cups beef stock

2 large onions - finely chopped

1/2 cup dried apricots - cut in half

1/4 cup dates - cut in half

1/4 cup raisins

1/4 cup flaked almonds

2 tablespoons olive oil

2 tablespoons fresh parsley - chopped

1 tablespoon clear honey

3 cloves garlic - crushed

1 teaspoon saffron stamens - soaked in cold water

Combine the following ingredients in a small bowl:

1 ½ tablespoons paprika

1 ½ tablespoons ground ginger

1 tablespoon turmeric

2 teaspoons ground cinnamon

2 teaspoons ground black pepper

1 teaspoon cayenne pepper

Directions:

1. Place lamb in a large bowl and toss with half the small bowl mix. Refrigerate for at least 6 hours - overnight is better.

2. Heat oil in a large skillet over medium heat. Add lamb and onion, cook till lamb is browned. Add remaining small bowl mix and garlic, mix well.

3. Add the beef stock, tomato juice, canned tomatoes, apricots, dates, raisins, almonds, honey and saffron to the skillet. Gently bring to a boil.

4. Transfer skillet contents to a casserole dish, and cover.

5. Put casserole dish in a **preheated 300 degree oven** and cook for 1 hour 50 minutes, or till meat is tender. Garnish with chopped parsley before serving.

Adding tangerines to a green salad goes well with this Moroccan lamb tagine.

Traditional Lamb Stew

Prep: 15 min - Cook: 60 min – Serves Four

Ingredients:

1½ lb. lamb – trimmed - cut into 1½ inch chunks

1¾ cups beef broth

4 small potatoes – peeled and cubed

3 large onions – quartered

3 medium carrots – cut into 1-inch pieces

2 tablespoons olive oil

1 tablespoon butter

1 tablespoon all-purpose flour

1½ teaspoons fresh parsley – minced

1½ teaspoons chives – minced

1/2 teaspoon fresh thyme – minced

1/2 teaspoon fresh rosemary – minced

1/2 teaspoon salt

1/4 teaspoon ground black pepper

Directions:

1. In a skillet, heat 1 tablespoon olive oil over medium heat, add meat, brown on all sides, about five minutes.

Remove meat and set to side.

2. Add onions, carrots and remaining oil to the pan, cook till onions are tender, stirring often, then add broth, lamb, potato, salt and pepper. Bring to a boil, then lower heat to simmer. Cover and simmer for 45 minutes or till meat is tender, stirring occasionally.

3. With a slotted spoon, remove meat and vegetables to a large bowl and pour pan juices into another bowl. Add parsley, chives, thyme and rosemary to bowl with pan juices. Set bowls to side.

4. In the skillet, melt butter over medium heat, then gradually add in flour, stirring till smooth. Slowly whisk in pan juices and cook till thickened, about 3 minutes. Add meat and vegetables, turn off heat.

5. Cover pan and let sit a few minutes before serving.

A green salad and bread rolls compliment this stew.

Mongolian Lamb

Prep: 15 min - Cook: 15 min – Serves Four

Ingredients:

1 lb. lamb fillet – trimmed – cut into thin strips

4 spring onions - julienned

1 carrot - julienned

1/3 cup dry sherry

2 tablespoons olive oil

3 tablespoons soy sauce

3 tablespoons sweet chili sauce

2 cloves garlic - crushed

1 teaspoon sesame seeds - toasted

Directions:

1. Heat 1 tablespoon olive oil in a skillet over medium heat, add lamb and stir-fry for 3 minutes. Remove lamb from skillet.

2. Add the remaining 1 tablespoon of olive oil to skillet. Heat, then add the spring onion, carrot and garlic. Stir-fry for 2 minutes, then remove from skillet.

3. Add sherry, soy sauce and chili sauce to skillet, bring to boil, then reduce heat and simmer for 3 minutes, sauce

will thicken.

4. Return the lamb, spring onion, garlic and carrots to the skillet. Toss to coat with sauce.

5. Sprinkle with sesame seeds and serve.

White rice, green salad and bread rolls compliment this Mongolian lamb dish.

Easy Lamb Pilaf

Prep: 10 min - Cook: 25 min – Serves Four

Ingredients:

1½ lb. boneless lamb – trimmed - cut into 1½ inch chunks

1 large onion - chopped

2 tablespoons parsley - chopped

1 tablespoon fresh mint leaves - chopped

1 tablespoon pine nuts - toasted

1 tablespoon olive oil

Combine the following ingredients in a bowl:

2 cups lamb stock

1¾ cups basmati rice

8 oz. can diced tomato

1 cup raisins

2 garlic cloves - crushed

1 tablespoon mild curry powder

1/4 teaspoon salt

Directions:

1. Put oil in skillet over medium heat, add onion and sauté 2 minutes, add lamb and sauté 2 more minutes till meat is

browned.

2. Stir in the bowl ingredients and bring to the boil, lower heat, cover and simmer for 20 minutes.

3. Remove from heat and let stand for 5 minutes. Stir in the parsley and mint, then sprinkle top with pine nuts, and serve.

Naan bread and a green salad go very well with this lamb pilaf.

Roast Rack of Lamb

Prep: 5 min – Marinate: 60 min - Cook: 25 min – Serves Four

Ingredients:

1 (8 bone) rack of lamb

Combine the following ingredients in a small bowl:

1½ tablespoons Dijon mustard

1 tablespoon fresh rosemary - chopped

1 tablespoon fresh thyme - chopped

1 garlic cloves - minced

1 tablespoon balsamic vinegar

1 tablespoon olive oil

1/2 teaspoon kosher salt

Directions:

1. Brush the lamb with small bowl mix; refrigerate one hour.

2. Put rack of lamb in a baking dish.

3. Place baking dish in a **preheated 425 degree oven**. Roast lamb for 25 minutes for medium rare. Remove from oven, cover and let sit for 5 minutes.

4. Cut in between the bone to slice into 8 chops. Serve immediately.

Garlic mashed potato, green beans and mint jelly makes this the perfect dish.

Honey Lemon Thyme Lamb Chops

Prep: 5 min - Cook: 25 min – Serves Four

Ingredients:

4 Lamb chops

1/2 cup honey

1/2 cup fresh lemon juice

1/4 cup olive oil

3 tablespoons thyme leaves - fresh - chopped

1 tablespoon Dijon mustard

1 garlic clove - crushed

1/2 teaspoon kosher salt

1/2 teaspoon crushed red pepper flakes

Directions:

1. In a small saucepan, combine honey, lemon juice, olive oil, thyme, mustard, garlic, salt and pepper flakes. Heat till it begins to simmer, then remove from heat immediately, allow to cool.

2. Pierce lamb chops several times with a fork. Place chops in a plastic food storage bag and add 3/4 of marinade from saucepan. Marinate in refrigerator for 4 to 24 hours. Put remaining marinade in a container and refrigerate.

3. Remove chops from bag, brown chops both sides in a skillet for 2 - 3 minutes. Transfer chops to a baking sheet.

4. Put baking sheet in a **preheated 425 degree oven** for 15 minutes, or till desired doneness.

5. Reheat reserved marinade and brush chops just before serving.

A baked potato, green vegetable and green salad complete this tasty dish.

Slow-Roasted Leg of Lamb and Potatoes

Prep: 15 min - Cook: 4 hours – Serves Six

Ingredients:

5 lb. leg of lamb

3 lb. potatoes - peeled - cut into 1/4 inch slices

2 lb. tomatoes - cut into 1/4 inch slices

2 medium onions - cut into 1/4 inch slices

2 cups dry white wine

1/3 cup olive oil

4 fresh bay leaves

Kosher salt and black pepper to taste

Combine the following ingredients in a small bowl:

4 garlic cloves - crushed

2 tablespoons fresh thyme leaves

1 tablespoon kosher salt

Directions:

1. Place lamb in a large roasting pan, rub lamb with small bowl mix.

2. Layer potatoes, tomatoes, and then onion around and up sides of lamb.

3. Season with salt and pepper.

4. Drizzle oil over lamb and vegetables, add wine and bay leaves. Cover pan with foil.

5. Roast lamb in a **preheated 350 degree oven** for 3½ hours.

6. Remove foil, **increase oven temperature to 425 degree**. Continue to roast lamb in oven for 25 minutes. Remove from oven and let stand 15 minutes.

7. Pull meat from bone in large chunks, discard bone and fat.

8. Place meat and vegetables on a platter.

9. Skim fat from juices in pan and discard. Put juices in a gravy jug and serve with the lamb.

Greek Style Lamb Burgers with salad topping

Prep: 10 min - Cook: 10 min – Serves Four

Ingredients:

1 tablespoon olive oil

4 hamburger buns

Combine the following ingredients in a bowl to make burgers:

1½ lb. lamb - ground

1 small onion - minced

1 garlic clove - minced

3 tablespoons fresh mint - finely chopped

3 tablespoons fresh parsley - finely chopped

1/2 teaspoon salt

1/4 teaspoon ground black pepper

Combine the following ingredients in a bowl to make salad:

1 cup feta - crumbled

4 lettuce leaves - shredded

1 tomato - thinly sliced

1 red onion - thinly sliced

2 tablespoons olive oil

1 tablespoon apple cider vinegar

Directions:

1. Heat oil in skillet over medium-high heat.

2. Divide lamb mix and shape into 4 patties. Cook lamb burgers 4 minutes on each side for medium, or longer till desired tenderness.

3. Toast buns under broiler.

4. Place burger on each bun then top with salad.

5. Serve immediately.

Lamb Gyros

Prep: 20 min - Cook: 45 min – Serves Four

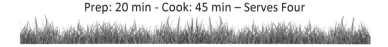

Ingredients:

4 pita bread

2 tomatoes - chopped

1 red onion - finely sliced

Combine the following ingredients in a bowl:

1 lb. lamb - ground

6 bacon slices – fat removed - chopped

1/2 cup scallions - chopped

1 tablespoon fresh oregano - chopped

1 tablespoon fresh mint - chopped

2 garlic cloves – minced

2 teaspoons fresh rosemary

1 teaspoon kosher salt

1/4 teaspoon ground black pepper

Combine the following ingredients to make tzatziki sauce:

1 cup Greek yogurt

1 medium cucumber - peeled - seeded - chopped

2 tablespoons lemon juice

1/2 teaspoon kosher salt

1/4 teaspoon ground black pepper

Directions:

1. Prepare the tzatziki sauce and refrigerate.

2. Prepare bowl ingredients as listed above, then combine.

3. Transfer bowl ingredients to a food processor, process into a smooth paste, about 1 minute.

4. Shape the lamb paste into a rectangle about 8X5 on a baking sheet.

5. Bake lamb in a **preheated 300 degree oven** for 40 minutes. Remove, and let stand for 10 minutes.

6. Slice the lamb making thin strips. Put the strips back on the baking tray.

7. Broil lamb strips till browned, about 2 minutes.

8. Heat the pita bread till warmed. Top each pita with lamb, tomato, onion and tzatziki sauce.

9. Wrap in foil and serve.

Tandoori Leg of Lamb

Prep: 20 min – Marinate: 24 hours – Cook: 2 hours - Serves Six

Ingredients:

5 lb. leg of lamb

1 cup yogurt - low fat

Combine the following ingredients in a small bowl:

1/4 cup fresh lime juice

1 tablespoon fresh garlic - minced

1 tablespoon lime zest - grated

1 tablespoon fresh ginger - grated

2 teaspoons kosher salt

1½ teaspoons paprika

1½ teaspoons coriander

1 teaspoon cumin

1 teaspoon turmeric

1/2 teaspoon cardamom

1/2 teaspoon mustard powder

1/2 teaspoon cayenne pepper

1/8 teaspoon ground cloves

1/8 teaspoon cinnamon

1/4 teaspoon black pepper

Directions:

1. With a sharp knife, make 1/4-inch to 1/2-inch-deep gashes on all sides of lamb in a crisscross pattern.

2. Prepare small bowl ingredients with 2 tablespoons of yogurt to make a paste. Rub paste into lamb.

3. Place lamb in a roasting pan, pour yogurt over lamb and gently pat sides with yogurt. Cover with plastic wrap and refrigerate for 24 hours.

4. Remove plastic wrap from lamb and bake uncovered in a **preheated 375 degree oven** for 1 hour 40 minutes (medium rare) or longer, till desired tenderness.

5. Remove from oven and let stand for 10 minutes.

6. Save juices from pan and serve with lamb.

Rice, naan and green salad compliments tandoori lamb. Finish dinner with ice cream and fruit salad.

Spicy Sichuan Lamb

Prep: 10 min – Rest: 10 min - Cook: 15 min – Serves Four

Ingredients:

1½ lb. lamb fillet – trimmed - thinly sliced

1 large white onion - cut into 2 inch pieces

2 scallions - thinly sliced

1/2 cup cilantro leaves

1/4 cup chicken broth - low sodium

1 tablespoon olive oil

Combine the following ingredients into a large bowl:

2 tablespoons olive oil

2 tablespoons ground cumin

1 tablespoon soy sauce

1 tablespoon cornstarch

2 teaspoons sesame oil

1½ teaspoons crushed red pepper

1 teaspoon sugar

Kosher salt and ground black pepper to taste

Directions:

1. Combine bowl ingredients, let rest for 10 minutes.

2. Heat olive oil in a skillet over medium-high heat. Sauté the lamb and onion for 10 minutes, or until browned.

3. Stir in the scallions, cilantro and broth. Cook till broth has evaporated, about 3 minutes.

4. Serve immediately.

Serve with rice.

Lamb Chops with Rosemary and Grapes

Prep: 5 min - Cook: 25 min – Serves Four

Ingredients:

8 lamb chops

2 cups red seedless grapes

1/3 cup dry white wine

3 tablespoons fresh rosemary - chopped

1½ tablespoons olive oil

4 garlic cloves - sliced

1 teaspoon honey

Kosher salt and black ground pepper to taste

Directions:

1. Season the chops with salt and pepper.

2. In a large skillet, heat oil over medium heat. Add the chops and 1 tablespoon of rosemary. Cook chops for 5 minutes on both sides for medium rare. Remove chops, cover, and place in warm oven. Keep juices in skillet.

3. Add the grapes and garlic to skillet, reduce heat to low, cook grapes till they soften, about 8 minutes.

4. Add wine and rosemary to skillet and simmer for 3 minutes. Remove from heat and add the honey.

5. Arrange chops on plates and top with the grape sauce.

6. Serve immediately.

Potato or rice with a green vegetable complete this tasty dish.

Lamb Rogan Josh

Prep: 20 min - Cook: 82 min – Serves Six

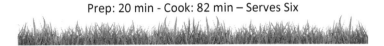

Ingredients:

2 lb. boneless lamb – trimmed - cut into 1½ inch chunks

2 red peppers - thinly sliced

2 onions - thinly sliced

2 cups water

1 cup yogurt - low fat

1/4 cup tomato puree

1/4 cup olive oil

2 tablespoons fresh ginger - peeled - grated

2 tablespoons fresh mint - chopped

1 tablespoon plus 1 teaspoon Madras curry powder

3 garlic cloves - minced

1 teaspoon turmeric

1 teaspoon cayenne

2 bay leaves

1 teaspoon garam masala

Kosher salt

Directions:

1. Heat the oil in a skillet over medium high heat. Add the lamb, season with salt and cook till lamb is browned, about 12 minutes. Remove lamb from skillet and set to side.

2. Add the onions and peppers to skillet and cook over medium heat till browned, about 4 minutes.

3. Add the ginger, garlic, curry, turmeric, cayenne and bay leaves and cook for 2 minutes.

4. Add the tomato puree, yogurt and water, bring to a boil. Add the lamb and any juices. Cover and simmer for one hour.

5. Stir in the garam masala, cook for 4 minutes.

6. Serve immediately, garnish with chopped mint.

Basmati rice and naan complete this authentic Indian dish.

Braised Lamb Chops with Red Wine and Fruit

Prep: 20 min - Cook: 3 hours – Serves Four

Ingredients:

4 lamb chops

2 onions - halved - sliced

3 tablespoons olive oil

Combine the following ingredients in a small bowl:

1 cup red wine

1/2 cup beef broth

1/4 cup dried cherries - chopped

1/4 cup dried apricots - chopped

3 tablespoons Dijon mustard

1 tablespoon rosemary - fresh - chopped

4 garlic cloves - minced

1 teaspoon kosher salt

1/2 teaspoon ground black pepper

Directions:

1. Put 2 tablespoons of oil and onion in a skillet, cook over medium-high heat till onions are browned. Remove onion from skillet, and set to side.

2. Add remaining 1 tablespoon of oil to skillet over medium heat. Add chops and cook 4 minutes on each side, till browned.

3. Return the onion to the skillet, and add the bowl mix. Bring to boil, then remove from heat.

4. Transfer skillet ingredients to a baking pan. Cover tightly with foil.

5. Braise in a **preheated 300 degree oven** for 2½ hours, or till chops are tender.

6. Remove from oven and let stand for 10 minutes.

7. Serve immediately.

Garlic mashed potato and green beans compliment this dish.

Grilled Turkish Ground Lamb Kebabs

Prep: 10 min - Chill: 60 min – Cook: 10 min - Serves Six

Ingredients:

6 pita bread

2 tomatoes - thinly sliced

1 red onion - thinly sliced

1 cup parsley leaves - fresh

Pickled sport peppers

Combine the following ingredients in a large bowl:

1lb. boneless lamb – trimmed - ground

2 teaspoons sumac - ground

1 tablespoon Urfa pepper flakes - ground

2 tablespoons cold water

1½ teaspoons kosher salt

1 teaspoon cumin - ground

Combine the following ingredients in a small bowl:

2 teaspoons sumac - ground

2 teaspoons Urfa pepper flakes - ground

1 teaspoon kosher salt

1 teaspoon cumin - ground

Directions:

1. Combine large bowl ingredients, adding cold water last. Knead well by hand, cover bowl and refrigerate for 1 hour.

2. Prepare small bowl ingredients and set to side.

3. Divide lamb mixture into 12 even size balls. Form each ball into a long flat kebab around a skewer.

4. Place kebabs on a **preheated hot grill**. Sprinkle kebabs with small bowl mix during grilling, turn kebabs occasionally. Total grilling time should be approximately 10 minutes.

5. Heat pitas on grill.

6. Serve hot kebabs with warm pita, tomatoes, onion, parsley and pickled peppers.

Lamb and Vegetable Stir-Fry

Prep: 15 min - Cook: 20 min - Serves Six

Ingredients:

1 lb. lamb fillet – trimmed - cut into thin strips

3 cups cabbage - shredded

3 carrots - julienned

2 celery stalks - julienned

1 cup snow peas

1 cup mushrooms - sliced

1 can water chestnuts (8 oz.) - sliced - drained

6 green onions - sliced

1 red bell pepper - chopped

1 tablespoon olive oil

1 tablespoon sesame seeds - toasted

1 tablespoon fresh ginger - minced

2 garlic cloves - minced

Combine the following ingredients in a small bowl:

1/4 cup soy sauce

2 tablespoons red wine

1 tablespoon cornstarch

1/4 teaspoon ground black pepper

1/8 teaspoon cayenne

Directions:

1. Combine small bowl ingredients, set to side.

2. Toast seeds in skillet over medium high heat, remove and set to side.

3. Add oil to skillet and heat. Sauté the lamb in hot oil for 3 minutes, add carrots, celery and mushrooms to lamb, sauté for 3 minutes. Remove all skillet ingredients and set to side.

4. Reduce heat to medium-low; add small bowl mix to skillet, stir till mix begins to thicken. Add lamb and vegetables, onion, cabbage, snow peas, chestnuts, garlic, ginger and red peppers, increase heat to medium high, sauté for 3 – 5 minutes, or till desired tenderness.

5. Serve immediately, sprinkle with toasted seeds.

Grilled Lamb Chops with Mint-Mango Sauce

Prep: 5 min - Cook: 12 min - Serves Four

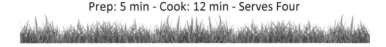

Ingredients:

8 Lamb chops

Combine the following ingredients in a blender to make Mango Sauce:

1 cup ripe mango - chopped

1/4 cup fresh mint - chopped

2 green onions - chopped

1 tablespoon fresh jalapeño pepper - seeded - chopped

1 tablespoon fresh lime juice

1 tablespoon fresh lemon juice

Combine the following ingredients in a small bowl:

1 tablespoon brown sugar

1 teaspoon ground cumin

1 teaspoon ground black pepper

2 garlic cloves - minced

1/2 teaspoon kosher salt

Directions:

1. Blend mango sauce ingredients till smooth. Place sauce in a bowl, cover and refrigerate.

2. Coat chops with small bowl mix. **Grill over medium heat** for 6 minutes each side, or longer till desired tenderness.

3. Put 1 tablespoon of mango sauce on each serving plates, place chops to the side of sauce.

4. Serve immediately.

A baked potato and green beans complete this delicious dinner.

Roasted Vegetable Irish Lamb Stew

Prep: 15 min - Cook: 2 hours – Serves Six

Ingredients:

3 lb. boneless lamb – trimmed - cut into 1½ inch chunks

3 cups beef stock

2 cups leeks - sliced

1/2 cup flour

4 ounces unsalted butter

1 cup Guinness beer

1 cup tomatoes - peeled - diced

1 cup mushrooms - sliced

1/2 lb. turnip - peeled and cut into 2-inch pieces

1/2 lb. potatoes - peeled and cut into 2-inch pieces

1/2 lb. carrots - peeled and cut into 2-inch pieces

4 tablespoons olive oil

4 garlic cloves - cut in half

2 teaspoons fresh rosemary - chopped

Kosher salt and fresh ground black pepper

Directions:

1. Heat 2 tablespoon of olive oil in a pot over medium-high heat, add the lamb and brown. Remove lamb and set to side.

2. Add leeks to pan and sauté till soft, add butter and melt, then add flour to make a roux. Turn heat down to low and cook till roux is brown, about 10 minutes.

3. Mix in the beer, stock, tomatoes, mushrooms and lamb. Bring to a simmer and cover. Simmer for 90 minutes.

4. Combine the potatoes, turnip, carrots, 2 tablespoons olive oil, garlic, rosemary, and salt and pepper to taste in a large bowl.

5. Place the vegetables in a roasting pan and roast in a **preheated 400 degree oven** for 45 minutes.

6. Add the roasted vegetables to the lamb. Simmer an additional 10 minutes. Remove from heat, season with salt and pepper if needed. Let stand 5 minutes before serving.

Marinated Grilled Lamb Kebabs

Prep: 15 min - Marinate: 2 hours - Cook: 10 min - Serves Six

Ingredients:

3 lb. boneless lamb – trimmed – 1½ inch cubes

15 ounces coconut milk

1 pint cherry tomatoes

2 onions - cut into 2-inch squares

8oz white button mushrooms

1 red bell pepper - cut into 2-inch squares

1 green bell pepper - cut into 2-inch squares

1 orange bell pepper - cut into 2-inch squares

2 tablespoons apple cider vinegar

2 tablespoons olive oil

Kosher salt and fresh ground black pepper

Skewers

Directions:

1. In a bowl, combine lamb, milk and vinegar, cover and refrigerate for 2 hours.

2. Remove lamb from bowl, gently pat lamb dry with paper towel.

3. Assemble the kebabs: fill skewers, alternating peppers, lamb, tomatoes, onions and mushrooms until all ingredients are used.

4. **Preheat heat grill to medium**. Season kebabs with salt and pepper, then grill kebabs on all sides, rotating every few minutes until desired tenderness, about 10 minutes.

5. Serve immediately.

Orange Roast Lamb and Potatoes

Prep: 10 min - Cook: 60 min - Serves Six

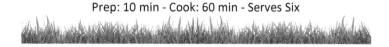

Ingredients:

3 lb. butterflied leg of lamb – trimmed

12 potatoes - peeled and cut into 2 inch cubes

5 garlic cloves

Combine the following ingredients in a large bowl:

4 tablespoons Dijon mustard

1/4 cup orange juice

3 tablespoons olive oil

1 tablespoon oregano

Kosher salt and fresh ground black pepper

Directions:

1. Whisk the bowl ingredients, then add the potato cubes to the bowl, mix well to coat potatoes.

2. Transfer potatoes to a roasting pan.

3. Cut 5 slits into the lamb, and stuff slits with garlic cloves. Place lamb in bowl and coat with mixture.

4. Transfer lamb to roasting pan, place on top of potatoes. Pour over any remaining mixture from bowl.

5. Baked uncovered in a **preheated 350 degree oven** for 60 minutes, or till desired tenderness.

6. Let sit for 10 minutes before serving.

A green or fruit salad compliments this delicious main course.

Roast Leg of Lamb with Ginger and Roast Potatoes

Prep: 10 min - Cook: 2.5 hours - Serves Six

Ingredients:

5 lb. leg of lamb

2 lb. new potatoes - small - cleaned - do not peel

3 tablespoons maple syrup

1 tablespoon olive oil

1 teaspoon fresh rosemary

Kosher salt and fresh ground black pepper

Combine the following ingredients in a small bowl:

1 tablespoon fresh ginger - peeled - minced

1 tablespoon fresh mint - chopped

1 tablespoon olive oil

1 teaspoon fresh rosemary

Directions:

1. Make 1/2 inch slits in the lamb and stuff holes with small bowl mix. Put lamb on a rack in a roasting pan.

2. Place pan in a **preheated 375 degree oven** and roast for 90 minutes.

3. Add 1 tablespoon olive oil and potatoes to a bowl, stir to coat potatoes with oil. Add potatoes to the roasting pan, sprinkle rosemary, salt and pepper over potatoes. Return to oven, roast for 30 minutes.

4. Remove baking pan from oven, glaze lamb with 1/2 maple syrup. Return to oven, roast for 10 minutes. Coat lamb again with remaining syrup, roast 10 minutes, remove from oven, Let stand 15 minutes before serving.

5. Serve on a platter with the roasted potatoes.

Adding your favorite vegetable completes this main course.

Roast Leg of Lamb with Apricot Glaze

Prep: 10 min - Cook: 2 hours - Serves Six

Ingredients:

5 lb. leg of lamb

1 cup dried apricots

4 tablespoons fresh mint

3 tablespoons honey

1 tablespoon olive oil

1 tablespoon fresh ginger

Kosher salt and black pepper to taste

Directions:

1. Place lamb in a roasting pan, rub lamb with oil, season with salt and pepper.

2. Put lamb in a **preheated 375 degree oven**, roast for 90 minutes.

3. Put apricots in a bowl, cover apricots with boiling water, set to side for 1 hour.

4. Drain apricots and put in a food processor along with the mint, honey and ginger. Blend well.

5. Remove lamb from oven after 90 minutes and spread apricot glaze evenly over top of lamb. Return to oven and roast 30 minutes.

6. Remove lamb from oven and let stand 15 minutes before serving.

Mashed potato and your favorite vegetable complete this main course.

British Lamb Hotpot

Prep: 20 min - Cook: 1 hour 40 min - Serves Four

Ingredients:

2 lb. boneless lamb – trimmed - cut into 1½ inch chunks

2 lbs. potatoes - peeled and sliced

2 cups and 3 tablespoons chicken stock

8 tablespoons butter - melted

4 carrots - peeled and sliced

2 medium onions - chopped

1½ tablespoons flour

2 teaspoons Worcestershire sauce

1 teaspoon fresh rosemary

2 bay leaves

Kosher salt and black pepper to taste

Directions:

1. Melt 3 tablespoons of butter in a skillet over medium heat. Add the lamb and brown for 5 minutes. Remove lamb from skillet and set to side.

2. Sauté the carrots and onions in skillet for 3 minutes, add more butter if needed. Sprinkle flour over onion and carrots, stir well, and cook 2 minutes. Add stock, Worcestershire sauce, lamb, rosemary and bay leaves, bring to boil, then remove from heat.

3. Transfer skillet contents to a casserole dish. Arrange the sliced potato on top of meat. Season top of potato with salt and pepper, and drizzle with melted butter.

4. Cover casserole dish and put in a **preheated 325 degree oven** for 90 minutes. Remove cover, brush potatoes with remaining butter. Cook under broiler till potatoes brown.

5. Let stand 5 minutes before serving.

Indian Lamb Curry

Prep: 10 min - Cook: 80 min - Serves Four

Ingredients:

1½ lbs. boneless lamb – trimmed - cut into 1½ inch chunks

14 oz. can diced tomatoes

1/3 cup Greek yogurt

1/4 cup olive oil

1/4 cup water

2 onions - medium - finely chopped

2 tablespoons fresh cilantro leaves - chopped

1 tablespoon fresh ginger paste

2 teaspoons coriander powder

1½ teaspoons garam masala

1 teaspoon cayenne pepper

1/2 teaspoon turmeric

2 garlic cloves - minced

1 green chili pepper - chopped

10 peppercorns

4 whole cloves

2 bay leaves

1 black cardamom pod

1 cinnamon stick

1/4 teaspoon kosher salt

Directions:

1. Heat oil in skillet over medium-high heat, add lamb, brown on all sides, about 5 minutes. Remove lamb and set to side.

2. Add bay leaves, cardamom, cinnamon stick, peppercorns, and cloves to the skillet. Cook for 1 minute, then add the onion and sauté for 10 minutes.

3. Stir in 2 tablespoons water, ginger paste, garlic, chili pepper, salt, and then lamb. Lower heat to medium, cook for 20 minutes, stirring often.

4. Add turmeric, coriander powder, cayenne, garam masala and 1/4 cup of water. Stir well, cook for 5 minutes. Add tomato, cook for 5 minutes, stirring often.

5. Stir in 1 cup of water and simmer for 30 minutes. Slowly stir in yogurt, simmer till lamb is tender.

6. Garnish with cilantro and serve immediately.

White rice and Naan bread are highly recommended with this dish.

Greek Lamb Salad

Prep: 15 min - Cook: 10 min - Serves Six

Ingredients:

2 lbs. lamb fillet – trimmed – cut into slices

1/2 cup Worcestershire sauce

2 tablespoons olive oil

ground black pepper

3/4 cup black olives

3/4 cup crumbled feta cheese

Combine the following ingredients to make Salad:

1 lettuce - romaine - torn into bite-size pieces

1 cup cherry tomatoes - halved

1 English cucumber - peeled and chopped

1 medium red onion - cut into thin rings

1 green pepper - cut into thin rings

Combine the following ingredients to make Dressing:

6 tablespoons olive oil

1 1/2 tablespoons fresh lemon juice

1 tablespoon apple cider vinegar

2 garlic cloves - minced

1 teaspoon oregano - dried

Directions:

1. Whisk together salad dressing, set to side.

2. Make salad, add dressing and toss. Set to side.

3. Toss the lamb in the Worcestershire sauce, then remove and season lamb with ground black pepper.

4. Heat oil in skillet over high heat. Cook the lamb, turning over occasionally, for 7 minutes or desired tenderness is reached. Remove lamb, set to side.

5. Arrange salad on plates, top salad with lamb, then sprinkle olives and cheese over salad. Serve immediately.

Scottish Shepherd's Pie

Prep: 15 min - Cook: 45 min - Serves Four

Ingredients:

1 lb. lamb – trimmed - minced

1½ lb. potatoes

1 onion – large - chopped

2 carrots - diced

1/4 cup mushrooms - sliced

1/4 cup cheddar cheese – shredded – low fat

1/4 cup milk – low fat

2 tablespoons butter

bay leaf

Kosher salt and ground black pepper

Combine the following ingredients in a small bowl:

1 cup beef broth

2 tablespoons flour - plain

1 tablespoon tomato paste

Directions:

1. Add the lamb, onion, mushrooms, carrots and bay leaf to a skillet (no oil), sauté 8 minutes over medium high heat.

2. Stir in the bowl mix, gently bring to a boil, then reduce heat, cover and simmer for 25 minutes.

3. Boil potatoes, drain well and mash with butter and milk. Season potato with salt and pepper to taste.

4. Transfer lamb to a casserole dish, cover lamb with potato, and sprinkle cheese over potato.

5. Bake in a **preheated 400 degree oven** for 20 minutes.

Serve with green vegetables and whole wheat bread rolls.

Roast Rack of Lamb

Prep: 10 min - Cook: 70 min - Serves Four

Ingredients:

1 (8 bone) rack of lamb - trimmed and frenched

2 tablespoons olive oil

1 tablespoon Dijon mustard

Combine the following ingredients in a small bowl:

1/2 cup fresh bread crumbs

2 tablespoons garlic - minced

2 tablespoons fresh rosemary - chopped

1/2 teaspoon black pepper

1/4 teaspoon kosher salt

2 tablespoons olive oil

Directions:

1. Combine small bowl ingredients, set to side.

2. Heat oil in a skillet over medium-high heat. Sear rack of lamb for 2 minutes each side. Remove from skillet.

3. Brush lamb with mustard, then evenly coat with bowl mix. Place coated lamb on a baking sheet.

4. Bake lamb in a **preheated 350 degree oven** for 45 minutes, then **increase oven to 400 degrees** for 15 minutes. Remove from oven.

5. Cut rack of lamb into individual ribs. Return to oven for 10 minutes.

6. Serve immediately.

Garlic mashed potato and green beans compliment this main course.

Grilled Lamb Burgers

Prep: 10 min - Chill: 20 min – Cook: 12 min - Serves Four

Ingredients:

4 hamburger rolls

4 romaine lettuce leaves

1 tomato - sliced

1 red onion - sliced

2 tablespoons Dijon mustard

Combine the following ingredients to make burgers:

1 lb. lamb – trimmed - minced

1 cup panko breadcrumbs

1 egg - beaten

2 tablespoons fresh mint leaves - chopped

1 tablespoon fresh oregano - chopped

1 shallot - minced

Directions:

1. Combine burger ingredients in a bowl, mix well. Shape into 4 burgers, cover and refrigerate for 20 minutes.

2. **Preheat grill to medium-high**, cook burgers 6 minutes each side, or till desired tenderness.

3. Grill inside of rolls. Spread mustard on toasted rolls, add burger and top with lettuce, tomato and onion. Serve immediately.

Grilled Kiwifruit Lamb Kebabs

Prep: 5 min - Marinate: 30 min - Cook: 12 min - Serves Eight

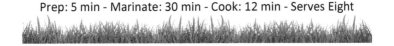

Ingredients:

2 lb. lamb - trimmed - cubed

2 kiwifruit - peeled – mashed

8 Skewers

Combine the following ingredients in a large bowl to make marinade:

2 tablespoons soy sauce

2 tablespoons sherry

1 tablespoon olive oil

2 garlic cloves - chopped

1/2 teaspoon sugar

1/4 teaspoon ground black pepper

Directions:

1. Combine marinade ingredients in a large bowl, add mashed kiwifruit and lamb. Cover and let sit at room temperature for 30 minutes.

2. Drain lamb and thread on skewers. **Preheat grill to medium high heat**. Grill kebabs 6 minutes, or longer till desired tenderness, turning often to brown and cook on all sides.

3. Serve immediately.

This goes very well served on top of a green salad with oil and vinegar dressing.

Lamb and Apricot Stew

Prep: 20 min - Marinate: 2 hours - Cook: 100 min - Serves Four

Ingredients:

2 lb. boneless lamb – trimmed - cut into 1½ inch chunks

1¼ cups chicken stock

3/4 cup dried apricots

2 fresh apricots - stoned - quartered

1/4 cup raisins

1/4 cup whole almonds

1/4 cup parsley - chopped

2 tomatoes - large - quartered

2 carrots - sliced

1½ tablespoons butter

1 onion - finely chopped

2 garlic cloves - finely chopped

1 cinnamon stick

2 teaspoons honey

Kosher salt

Combine the following ingredients in a bowl to make spice paste:

2 tablespoons chicken stock

4 whole green cardamom pods - crushed

1 teaspoon ground ginger

1 teaspoon cinnamon

1/4 teaspoon ground cloves

1/4 teaspoon ground coriander

1/4 teaspoon cayenne

1/4 teaspoon turmeric

ground black pepper to taste

Directions:

1. In a bowl, combine the spice paste ingredients, add lamb and coat with paste. Cover and refrigerate for 2 hours to marinate.

2. Melt butter in a skillet over medium heat. Add the onion, garlic and cinnamon stick, sauté till onions are soft.

3. Add the marinated lamb and chicken stock, cover and simmer for 80 minutes.

4. Add the apricots, raisins, almonds, tomatoes, carrots and honey. Simmer for 20 minutes or till lamb is cooked.

5. Add parsley and adjust seasoning before serving.

Leg of Lamb with Soy Honey

Prep: 10 min - Cook: 4 hours - Serves Six

Ingredients:

5 lb. leg of lamb

3 onions - sliced 1 inch thick

1¾ cups white wine

1 cup chicken stock

2 garlic cloves – minced

Combine the following ingredients in a small bowl to make soy honey glaze:

1/3 cup honey

3 tablespoons soy sauce

2 tablespoons fresh rosemary - chopped

1/2 teaspoon kosher salt

1/4 teaspoon ground black pepper

Directions:

1. Combine small bowl ingredients to make honey glaze. Set to side.

2. Line bottom of baking pan with onion slices, pour in the wine and stock, and sprinkle with garlic.

3. Place leg of lamb on top of onion. Brush lamb with half the honey glaze.

4. Roast lamb in a **preheated 400 degree oven** for 40 minutes. **Reduce oven temperature to 325 degrees**, brush lamb with remaining glaze, cover loosely with foil, and cook for 3 hours.

5. Remove lamb from oven and let sit covered for 15 minutes.

Serve slices of lamb with onion, garlic mashed potato and green beans. Top with pan juices.

Baked Lamb Samosas

Prep: 15 min - Cook: 20 min - Serves Six

Ingredients:

1 lb. boneless lamb – trimmed - minced

6 puff pastry sheets

1 cup frozen peas

1 cup mango chutney

1 onion - large - minced

1 carrot - grated

2 tablespoons tikka paste

2 tablespoons fresh mint - finely chopped

3 teaspoons olive oil

1/4 teaspoon kosher salt

1/8 teaspoon black pepper

Directions:

1. Heat 2 teaspoons of oil in a skillet over medium heat. Add the lamb, salt and pepper to skillet, sauté 5 minutes, or till meat is browned.

2. Mix in the tikka paste, combine well, and then add onion and carrot, sauté 5 minutes. Remove from heat and transfer lamb to a large bowl.

3. Add the frozen peas, 2 tablespoons of chutney and mint to bowl mix. Combine well, set to side to cool.

4. Cut pasty sheets into 5 inch pieces. Add 1 heaped tablespoon of lamb onto the pastry square. Dip finger in remaining teaspoon of olive oil, run finger around edges of pastry to moisten, fold in half to making a triangle, sealing lamb mix inside.

5. Brush samosas with oil, then place samosas on a baking sheet. Bake in a **preheated 350 degree oven** for 10 minutes. Turn over samosas, cook 10 minutes.

6. Serve immediately with remaining chutney on the side.

Your favorite green salad and/or fruit salad makes a wonderful brunch/dinner.

Lamb and Lima Bean Stew

Prep: 15 min - Cook: 2+ hours - Serves Six

Ingredients:

2 lb. boneless lamb – trimmed - cut into 1½ inch chunks

14 oz. can lima beans - drained

14 oz. can chopped tomatoes

2 cups chicken stock

1 cup red wine

2 onions - thickly sliced

4 carrots - julienned

4 tablespoons olive oil

3 tablespoons fresh rosemary - chopped

3 tablespoons balsamic vinegar

3 garlic cloves - finely chopped

1 red chili - deseeded - chopped

Directions:

1. Heat 2 tablespoons of oil in a skillet over medium heat. Add lamb and sauté till browned. Remove lamb from skillet and set to side.

2. Add remaining oil, onion and carrot to skillet, sauté 10 minutes. Stir in 2 tablespoon of rosemary, garlic, chili, tomatoes, stock, red wine and vinegar. Cook 5 minutes, stirring often.

3. Return lamb to skillet, lower heat and simmer for 2 hours. Stir in the lima beans and remaining rosemary, cook 10 minutes.

4. Serve immediately.

A green side salad and hearty bread compliments this delicious stew.

Baked Lamb Ribs

Prep: 15 min - Cook: 90 min - Serves Four

Ingredients:

2½ lb. lamb ribs

Kosher salt and ground black pepper

Combine the following ingredients in a small bowl:

2 tablespoons olive oil

1 tablespoon soy sauce

1 tablespoon tomato paste

2 garlic gloves - minced

Directions:

1. Make slits between ribs, place on a baking sheet, season with salt and pepper. Bake in a **preheated 350 degree oven** for 30 minutes. Turn ribs, baked another 30 minutes, then remove from oven.

2. Combine bowl ingredients well, making a paste; brush over ribs. Return ribs to oven for 30 minutes.

3. Cut ribs into serving pieces, serve immediately.

Perfect complement to your favorite salad.

Roast Lamb with Orange Mint Sauce

Prep: 15 min - Cook: 100 min - Serves Six

Ingredients:

3 lb. butterflied leg of lamb - trimmed

1 celery stick - finely chopped

1/4 cup blanched slivered almonds

1/4 cup chopped fresh mint

Combine following ingredients in a small saucepan:

1 can (6 oz.) frozen orange juice concentrate - thawed

1/4 cup lemon juice

1/4 cup butter

1/2 teaspoon salt

Directions:

1. Place lamb in a roasting pan. Roast in a **preheated 325 degree oven** for 45 minutes.

2. Heat saucepan ingredients, simmer for 6 minutes.

3. Brush lamb with orange juice mixture and continue to roast another 45 minutes, or till desired doneness.

4. Add celery to remaining orange juice mixture, simmer for 5 minutes. Stir in almonds and mint.

5. Serve lamb with sauce.

Lamb Chops Venetian-style

Prep: 15 min - Cook: 50 min - Serves Four

Ingredients:

4 lamb chops

1 medium eggplant - cut in half lengthwise - thinly sliced

8½ oz. can artichoke hearts

1 cup frozen peas

1 onion - medium – quartered

1 tablespoon olive oil

Kosher salt and ground black pepper

Combine the following ingredients in a small bowl:

1/2 cup water

3 tablespoons tomato paste

2 tablespoons olive oil

1 tablespoon fresh basil - chopped

Directions:

1. Heat oil in a skillet over medium heat. Season chops with salt and pepper, sauté 4 minutes each side, till browned. Remove chops, set to side.

2. Add onion to skillet and sauté 5 minutes, then add eggplant.

3. Stir in small bowl ingredients, bring to boil. Reduce heat to low, cover and simmer 15 minutes.

4. Add peas, artichokes and lamb chops. Cover and simmer 20 minutes.

5. Serve immediately.

Traditional Roast Leg of Lamb and Gravy

Prep: 5 min - Cook: 3 hours - Serves Eight

Ingredients:

5 lb. leg of lamb

2 teaspoons salt

1/4 teaspoon ground black pepper

Gravy ingredients:

2 cups water

2 tablespoons flour

1 tablespoon onion - minced

1 bay leaf

Directions:

1. Rub lamb with salt and pepper. Place lamb on rack in roasting pan.

2. Roast, uncovered in a **preheated 325 degree oven** for 3 hours for medium, or till desired tenderness.

3. Move lamb to a heated platter, keep warm.

4. Combine flour with 3 tablespoons of water, mix well, making a paste.

5. Pour pan drippings into a saucepan with remaining water, then flour paste. Slowly bring to a boil, stirring constantly, add onion and bay leaf. Lower heat and simmer for 5 minutes.

6. Serve immediately with the lamb.

Roast potato and roast vegetables are a treat with this traditional Sunday lunch recipe.

Lamb and Shrimp Kebabs

Prep: 15 min - Cook: 24 min - Serves Six

Ingredients:

1 tablespoon Olive oil

24 flat bamboo skewers*

Combine the following ingredients in a large bowl:

1¼ lb. lamb – trimmed - ground

1 lb. shrimp - peeled - deveined - finely chopped

1 cup red onion - finely chopped

1/4 cup fresh cilantro - finely chopped

1/4 cup fresh mint - finely chopped

4 garlic cloves - minced

1½ teaspoons kosher salt

1 teaspoon ground cumin

1/2 teaspoon red pepper flakes - crushed

1/2 teaspoon ground black pepper

Directions:

1. Combine bowl ingredients thoroughly.

2. Divide lamb and shrimp mix into 2 tablespoon pieces. Roll to make 2 inch long ovals.

3. Slide skewer into kebabs. Cover and chill till ready to use.

4. Heat oil in a skillet over medium-high heat. In batches, brown kebabs in skillet, about 2 minutes each side.

5. Place browned kebabs on a baking sheet. Roast kebabs in a **preheated 400 degree oven** for 20 minutes.

6. Serve immediately.

*Skip skewers, roll into balls to make lamb shrimp meatballs. Roast in oven 25 minutes

Grilled Lamb Loin Chops **with Rhubarb Chutney**

Prep: 15 min – Marinate: 20 Min - Cook: 30 min - Serves Four

Ingredients:

8 Lamb loin chops - trimmed

1/4 cup olive oil

2 tablespoons lemon juice

Kosher salt and black ground pepper

Rhubarb Chutney:

6 stalks rhubarb

1 leek - white part only - sliced thinly

1/2 cup orange juice

2 tablespoons red wine vinegar

2 tablespoons brown sugar

1 tablespoon olive oil

Directions:

1. Make chutney.

2. Combine oil and lemon juice, season to taste with salt and pepper.

3. Place chops on a flat dish or pan. Pour oil lemon marinade over chops. Cover and let stand for 20 minutes.

4. Preheat grill to medium high. Grill chops 3-4 minutes each side for medium rare, or longer until cooked as desired.

5. Serve immediately.

Directions:

1. Heat oil over medium high heat, in a saucepan. Add leek and sauté for 2 minutes. Add rhubarb, orange juice, vinegar and sugar, bring to a boil. Reduce heat and simmer 20 minutes.

2. Allow to cool a bit before serving with chops.

This is delicious with grilled vegetables.

Lamb Shanks in Red Wine Sauce

Prep: 15 min - Cook: 2 hours - Serves Four

Ingredients:

4 lamb shanks - trimmed

1 cup red wine

1/2 cup carrots - sliced

1/2 cup onions - sliced

1/2 cup celery – sliced

1/2 cup mushrooms

4 tablespoons olive oil

2 cloves garlic

1 teaspoon fresh thyme

1 teaspoon fresh rosemary

1/4 teaspoon crushed red pepper (optional)

Combine the following ingredients in a small bowl:

1 cup beef broth

2 teaspoons tomato paste

2 teaspoons plain flour

Directions:

1. Heat 2 tablespoons olive oil in a large saucepan, add shanks and brown all over, about 5 minutes. Remove from pan and set to side.

2. Add rest of olive oil to saucepan, then add the carrots, onions, mushrooms and celery, sauté till browned. Drain and discard oil in pan.

3. Stir in the red wine and small bowl mix, keep stirring slowly till liquid heats. Add garlic, thyme, rosemary and crushed red pepper, stir well. Add the shanks.

4. Cover pan and simmer 2 hours until tender and falling off the bone.

5. Skim sauce and reduce slightly to thicken (if necessary).

6. Serve immediately.

Creamy mashed potato and steamed vegetables complete this delicious lamb dish.

Indian Lamb Cutlets

Prep: 5 min - Cook: 12 min - Serves Four

Ingredients:

4 lamb cutlets

3/4 cup parmesan cheese - finely grated

1 tablespoon curry powder

1 tablespoon olive oil

Salt and ground black pepper to taste

Directions:

1. Combine parmesan and curry powder together, put mix on a flat plate.

2. Season lamb with salt and pepper, then press lamb into mix to coat.

3. Heat oil in an ovenproof pan and fry the cutlets for 2 minutes on each side to brown.

4. Transfer pan to a **preheated 375 degree oven** for 8 minutes (medium) or more till desired doneness.

5. Serve immediately.

Delicious served with tomato chutney and your favorite vegetables.

Lamb Chops with Kiwifruit

Prep: 5 min - Marinate: 4 hours - Cook: 24 min - Serves Four

Ingredients:

4 lamb chops

1 kiwifruit – peeled – mashed

1 kiwifruit - sliced – for garnish

Combine the following ingredients to make marinade:

1/2 cup olive oil

1/4 cup fresh oregano – chopped

2 garlic cloves – minced

1/4 teaspoon ground black pepper

Directions:

1. Combine marinade ingredients, mix well. Pour marinade into a large sealable plastic bag and add the lamb chops. Squeeze out the air, then seal the bag. Place bag in the refrigerator, and marinate 4 hours, or overnight.

2. Remove lamb from the marinade, cover with mashed kiwifruit, and let sit at room temperature for 10 minutes.

3. **Preheat grill to medium heat.** Grill chops 12 minutes each side, or till desired tenderness.

4. Garnish chops with kiwi slices and serve immediately.

Lamb Casserole

Prep: 15 min - Cook: 2 hours - Serves Six

Ingredients:

1½ lb. lamb – trimmed – cubed

3/4 cup frozen peas – thawed

3/4 cup carrots – julienned

3/4 cup hot water

1 lb. potatoes - cut in 1-inch pieces - cooked

1/2 cup onion - chopped

1/2 green bell pepper - chopped

1/2 cup celery - chopped

1/4 cup butter

1 tablespoon fresh parsley - chopped

1 teaspoon ground paprika

1/2 teaspoon fresh rosemary

Combine the following ingredients in a small bowl:

1/4 cup flour

1 1/2 teaspoons salt

1/4 teaspoon ground black pepper

Directions:

1. Coat lamb cubes in small bowl mix. Heat butter in skillet, add lamb and sauté till browned on all sides. Transfer lamb from skillet to casserole dish.

2. Add onion, green pepper and celery to skillet, sauté till onion is transparent, about 5 minutes. Transfer from skillet to casserole dish. **Stir contents and add Rosemary, paprika and hot water while stirring**

3. Cover and bake in a **preheated 350 degree oven** for 90 minutes. After 90 minutes, add the peas, carrots and potato. Continue to bake, uncovered, for 30 minutes – or till lamb is tender.

4. Garnish with parsley before serving.

Grilled Spicy Lamb Pitas

Prep: 10 min – Chill: 60 min - Cook: 10 min - Serves Eight

Ingredients:

8 medium pita breads – with pockets

Combine the following ingredients in a large bowl:

2½ lbs. lamb – trimmed - minced

1 cup shallots - finely chopped

3/4 cup fresh parsley - chopped

1/4 cup olive oil

1 tablespoon ground coriander

2 teaspoons kosher salt

1½ teaspoons ground black pepper

3/4 teaspoon ground cumin

1/2 teaspoon ground cinnamon

Directions:

1. Prepare bowl mix. Cover and refrigerate for 60 minutes.

2. Open each pita by cutting at the seam, cut just enough to spoon in lamb mix.

3. Spoon filling into pitas, carefully spread to edges. Close. Gently press top of pita with hand to ensure there is no air left inside. Pita will bond to lamb mix.

4. **Preheat grill to medium**. Grill pitas 5 minutes each side, or till filling is cooked, and bread is crisp.

Serve immediately.

Roast Leg of Lamb with Orange Juice and White Wine

Prep: 10 min - Marinate: 8 hours - Cook: 90 min - Serves Eight

Ingredients:

5 lb. leg of lamb – trimmed

Kosher salt

ground black pepper

Combine the following ingredients in a bowl to make marinade:

3/4 cup white wine

3/4 cup orange juice

1/4 cup olive oil

2 tablespoons fresh rosemary – chopped

2 tablespoons fresh thyme – chopped

2 garlic cloves - minced

1 teaspoon ground black pepper

Directions:

1. Combine marinade ingredients, mix well. Pour marinade into a large sealable plastic bag and add the lamb. Squeeze out the air, then seal the bag. Place bag in the refrigerator and marinate 8 hours, or overnight.

2. Remove lamb from the marinade and let sit at room temperature for 25 minutes. Pat lamb dry and season all over with salt and pepper. Place lamb on rack in roasting pan, fat side facing up.

3. Roast lamb in a **preheated 425 degree oven** for 30 minutes, then **reduce heat to 300 degrees**. Continue to roast for 60 minutes for medium rare, or longer till desired tenderness. Remove lamb from oven, cover loosely with foil, set to side for 15 minutes before serving.

You can add potatoes, and your choice of vegetables (I use whole carrots and onions) to the roasting pan, underneath the rack, when oven temperature is lowered to 300 degrees. For extra flavor, coat vegetables with the marinade.

Roast Lamb Shoulder with Pomegranate Glaze

Prep: 15 min - Cook: 3.5 hours - Serves Six

Ingredients:

1 lamb shoulder – about 3½ lb. - trimmed

1 large onion – thick slices

1 cup of water

Combine the following ingredients in a small bowl to make glaze:

1/4 cup of pomegranate molasses – homemade recipe below

1 lemon - juiced

1 tablespoon olive oil

1 teaspoon cumin

1/2 teaspoon red pepper flakes (optional)

3 garlic cloves – minced

Directions:

1. Cover bottom of baking pan with onion slices, pour in the water.

2. Place lamb on top of onion, pour glaze over lamb. Cover baking pan with foil.

3. Put the lamb in a **preheated 325 degree oven**, roast for 3 hours. Remove cover, and continue to roast for 30 minutes.

4. Pour off the juices from baking pan, set to side. Trim away as much fat as possible from the lamb, then pour juices back over lamb. Allow to rest for 15 minutes.

5. Serve lamb with sauce from pan.

Your favorite green salad with pomegranate seeds compliment this great tasting lamb shoulder.

Pomegranate Molasses:

2 cups pomegranate juice, 1/4 cup sugar, 2 tablespoons lemon juice

In a saucepan, heat the pomegranate juice, sugar and lemon juice. Once the sugar has dissolved, reduce heat to simmer. Simmer for about one hour, or until juice turns to a syrup consistency. Use remaining syrup over vanilla ice-cream for a lovely treat.

Curried Lamb Chops

Prep: 15 min - Cook: 20 min - Serves Four

Ingredients:

4 lamb chops

1 apple – cored - sliced – for garnish

1/2 cup apple – peeled – diced

1/2 cup onion - chopped

1 tablespoon olive oil

1/2 teaspoon curry powder

Combine the following ingredients in a bowl:

1¼ cups chicken broth

2 tablespoons lemon juice

1 tablespoon flour

1½ teaspoons Dijon mustard

1/2 teaspoon salt

1/2 teaspoon sugar

Directions:

1. In a skillet, heat oil, add chops and brown on both sides. Remove chops and set to side.

2. Add the onion, apple and curry to the skillet and sauté till onion is tender. Gradually stir in bowl ingredients. Bring to a boil, cook for 2 minutes. Lower heat.

3. Return chops to skillet, cover and simmer for 15 minutes or longer till desired tenderness, turning once.

4. Put chops on serving plates and top with sauce from skillet. Garnish with slice apple. Serve immediately.

Serve over a bed of rice with your favorite green vegetable on apple slices on the side.

Turkish Lamb Pizza *By Lauren Joe*

Prep: 15 min - Cook: 30 min - Serves Four

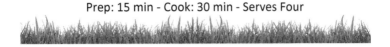

Ingredients:

3/4 lb. lamb – trimmed - minced

1 loaf Turkish bread or flat bread

1/2 cup cherry tomatoes - cut in half

1 medium onion - finely chopped

1/3 cup feta cheese

1/4 cup fresh parsley - chopped

2 tablespoons tomato paste

2 tablespoons pine nuts

1 tablespoon olive oil

1 tablespoon ground coriander

2 teaspoons ground cumin

1/2 teaspoon red pepper flakes - crushed

2 garlic cloves - minced

Kosher salt and ground black pepper

Directions:

1. Heat oil in a skillet over medium high heat, add onion and garlic. Sauté 3 minutes, then add lamb, coriander, cumin and red pepper flakes. Continue to sauté till meat is browned, about 5 minutes.

2. Add nuts, season to taste with salt and pepper, cook for 2 minutes. Remove from heat and set to side.

3. Place bread on a baking pan. Spread tomato paste onto bread, sprinkle with half the feta. Cover bread with lamb, sprinkle top with remaining feta.

4. Bake in a **preheated 375 degree oven** for 15 minutes. Top with tomato, broil 2 minutes.

5. Sprinkle with parsley, serve immediately.

International conversions:

Cooking Measurement Conversions

1 teaspoon = 1/6 fl. Ounce

1 Tablespoon = 1/2 fl. Ounce

1 tablespoon = 3 teaspoons

1 dessert spoon (UK) = 2.4 teaspoons

16 tablespoons = 1 cup

12 tablespoons = 3/4 cup

10 tablespoons + 2 teaspoons = 2/3 cup

8 tablespoons = 1/2 cup

6 tablespoons = 3/8 cup

5 tablespoons + 1 teaspoon = 1/3 cup

4 tablespoons = 1/4 cup

2 tablespoons = 1/8 cup

2 tablespoons + 2 teaspoons = 1/6 cup

1 tablespoon = 1/16 cup

2 cups = 1 pint

2 pints = 1 quart

3 teaspoons = 1 tablespoon

48 teaspoons = 1 cup

1 cup = 8 fluid ounces

2 cups= 1 pint

2 cups= 16 fluid ounces

1 quart = 2 pints

4 cups = 1 quart

4 cups = 32 fluid ounces

8 cups = 4 pints

8 cups = 1/2 gallon

8 cups = 64 fluid ounces

4 quarts =1 gallon

4 quarts = 128 fluid ounces

1 gallon (gal) = 4 quarts

16 ounces = 1 pound

Pinch = Less than 1/8 teaspoon

Fahrenheit to Celsius Degrees Conversions

225F = 110C = Gas mark 1/4

250F = 120C = Gas mark 1/2

275F = 140C = Gas mark 1

300F = 150C = Gas mark 2

325F = 160C = Gas mark 3

350F = 180C = Gas mark 4

375F = 190C = Gas mark 5

400F = 200C = Gas mark 6

425F = 220C = Gas mark 7

450F = 230C = Gas mark 8

475F = 240C = Gas mark 9

Imperial to Metric Conversions

1/4 teaspoon = 1.25 ml

1/2 tsp = 2.5 ml

1 tsp = 5 ml

1 tablespoon = 15 ml

1/4 cup = 60 ml

1/3 cup = 75 ml

1/2 cup = 125 ml

2/3 cup = 150 ml

3/4 cup = 175 ml

1 cup = 250 ml

1 1/8 cups = 275 ml

1 1/4 cups = 300 ml

1 1/2 cups = 350 ml

1 2/3 cups = 400 ml

1 3/4 cups = 450 ml

2 cups = 500 ml

2 1/2 cups = 600 ml

3 cups = 750 ml

3 2/3 cups = 900 ml

4 cups = 1 liter

Weight Conversion

1/2 oz = 15g

1 oz = 25 g

2 oz = 50 g

3 oz = 75 g

4 oz = 100 g

6 oz = 175 g

7 oz = 200 g

8 oz = 250 g

9 oz = 275 g

10 oz = 300 g

12 oz = 350 g

1 lb = 500 g

1 1/2 = 750 g

2 lb = 1 kg

Lamb.

½ Shoulder
Onion.
Oil
S & P.
Garlic

Rub lamb with oil then S+P/ Rosemary
cover with foil put in oven.
Stand to lamb on Onions

Oven 180° for 1½ hrs

Printed in Great Britain
by Amazon